I0192346

Pray for Donald Trump:

Help Make America Great Again by Supporting
the President of the United States of America's
Big Agenda through Powerful Specific
Fervent Intercessory Prayers

By: Patrick Baldwin

Copyright 2017

American Christian Defense Alliance, Inc.

Baltimore, Maryland

ACDAInc.Org

Special Request

Thank you for purchasing our book and supporting our Ministry. We actually have two requests – To Pray for Our Ministry and to Read this Book All the Way through. No Ministry can Survive without Prayers and Support so we ask you to keep our Ministry in Your Daily Prayers and Pray as the Lord leads.

We encourage you to Read the Book you purchased all the way through. Many Books NEVER Get Read, and the ones that do only get read the first few pages.

One of our Special Request is that if you are serious about learning the material in this book that you take time to actually read this book in its entirety – all the way through.

We all lead such busy lives nowadays and can get side tracked so easily, please take a moment to consider my words and read to the end of the book and keep us in Your Prayers.

Thank You once again for purchase. We deeply appreciate Your Prayers and Support and know that God will Bless You as You continue to Bless this Ministry.

Dedication:

This Book is dedicated to Donald J. Trump and His Family who have Courageously attempted to Make America Great Again. Words cannot express the Gratitude we as a Nation have for all you are attempting to do.

May the Lord Jesus Christ lead, guide, and protect you and your family from all enemies foreign or domestic, spiritual or physical, seen and unseen alike whether you are awake or sleeping. May the Lord Jesus Christ also protect you from yourself – Remember to lean not onto your own understanding but in all your ways acknowledge Him and He will direct you steps - Proverbs 3:4-6

Forward

The concept for this book developed because of Active Spiritual Warfare against Donald Trump and those that Support him that arose by witches and those that practice the dark arts.

For those that are unaware, in February 2017 media outlets worldwide indicated that witches would be conducting spiritual warfare against President Donald Trump and those that support him. Their end goal is to bind him and hinder him apparently from keeping his campaign promises to Make America Great Again. These witches plan to continue every month with the rituals until President Trump is no longer in office.

Now one has to ask themselves, "Why"? Why would witches and those that practice the occult and live in the United States not want to Make America Great Again?

Would not making America Great Again benefit them as well? Of course it would but for them there is a higher calling, for them bringing about the destruction of the United States is critical to ushering in their New World Order.

Furthermore it should be noted here that according to Larry Nichols (a former aide to the Clintons) Hillary Clinton is a practicing witch and has ties to a witch covenant in California. The combination of this information regarding Hillary Clinton's ties to a witch covenant and her well-known globalist positions seems to tie things together so we can start to understand how and why this assault even began.

Now I'm not sure about you but when I first heard about this I immediately thought about the Christian singer Carmen and his song, "Witches Invitation". If you've never heard the song I would encourage you to listen to it, or better yet watch the music video which is even better.

There's a saying, "There's no political solution to a spiritual problem". This quote is often accredited to Steve Quayle although others have set it as well. The reality is these witches and occult practitioners often times understand this better than Christians.

Many Christians believe that it was the Power of Prayer all across the nation by men and women of faith that enable Donald Trump to become President of the United States. To that I would agree.

However, many Christians don't stay in the fight, they feel that they did their part to get their guy elected and now it's up to him. Brothers and sisters this couldn't be further from the truth, we have to remain vigilant and diligent in our prayer life, especially if we truly want to Make America Great Again. Remember duties are ours results are up to God.

Although no nation has lasted forever it is through the power of prayer that we can move mountains but we must have faith, and what is faith but our expectations of what God is able to do. What does the Scriptures say, without faith it is impossible to please God. The Bible further declares the faith is the evidence of things unseen yet hope for. See faith is an action and so is love – and if we love Jesus we will follow him and do his commandments.

We know from the book of ecclesiastics that there is a time under heaven for everything – it is time to stand in the gap for President Trump and pray like never before.

Table of Contents

Chapter 1:
Is Donald Trump For or Against Us?

A lot of people wonder if President Donald Trump is for us or against us, is he a wolf in sheep's clothing or genuine patriot who wants to make America great again? Looking at things objectively there are no easy answers.

Let's look at things honestly and evaluate things openly to get a better perspective on it Is President Donald Trump for us or against us. Throw out your preconceived ideas, your assumptions, and whatever biases you may have within you and let's look at things together here for a moment.

Jesus said it best, "we will know them by their fruits". If we look at the fruit of President Donald Trump thus far what do we see? Do we see him keeping his campaign promises to the American people or do we see him wavering and going back on his promises – And if so Why?

Many people that have voted for him are very concerned with his actions thus far and those that he has appointed within his cabinet. A good portion of those that he is appointed to his cabinet could be considered globalist or technocrats. Is he part of the Technocracy Movement?

Others point to the financial ties between his son-in-law and a well-known globalist that is hell-bent on destroying America. The facts are the facts and whether we voted for him or not we must accept the reality of these facts and move forward in a productive way – I choose to pray.

The unfortunate reality of the connections between his son-in-law and the globalist billionaire allows for what is known as plausible deniability on the part of the President. Respectfully his son-in-law and daughter were not voted into office yet have tremendous influence over key policies and decisions. This should not be the case but nevertheless it is what it is.

I think the Godfather philosophy of keeping your friends close but your enemies closer only goes so far in the real world where lives hang in the balance of decisions on policies.

Again looking at things objectively we have to ask ourselves who is honestly qualified to fill these cabinet level positions and on board with the President's Big Agenda to Make America Great Again?

For me personally I can understand to some degree putting in the people that he has whether I like his choices are not, but then we come to his actions – has or is his actions mirroring his campaign promises? That my friend is still up for debate and is in part why this book is being written – that is to help support President Trump to fulfill his campaign promises to the American people by effectively intervening through the power of prayer on his behalf.

Make no mistake about it my friends President Trump has been targeted by those who practice the dark arts and want to destroy the United States of America. I personally attempt to do everything in my power to come against these dark forces through the power of prayer and faith in our Lord Jesus Christ, in whom we have the victory and the power over all demonic forces.

I truly hope you will join me in praying for President Trump and that you do your part to help Make America Great Again too.

What is the Measure of a Man . . . .

- The Heart

Chapter 2: Realistic Expectations

Let's talk about some realistic expectations now. Let's first look at the environment in which President Donald Trump has walked into. He's not really backed by the Republicans and is definitely not backed by the Democrats so who can he turn to for help when he needs it?

During the campaign both sides did everything in their power to try to destroy him but God through the faithful prayers of believers everywhere allowed Donald Trump to be our president for such a time as this - To help stand in the gap against the evil, the corruption, and the enemies of America.

Will you now when your president needs you most harden your heart and turn from him and refused to pray for him because you don't agree with something he said or did? Understand without you and me standing shoulder to shoulder with him in prayer the situation sure to get worse – remember," We The People".

So it's clear to see that President Trump has walked into a hostile work environment to say the least. He truly has enemies all around him, do you recognize that? I mean have you really thought about that? How would you perform in any job with enemies all around you seeking to sabotage and destroy the things that you're trying to accomplish? I would imagine that your morale and your motivation would take a serious hit – what do you think?

Remember, President Trump inherited an administration from Obama that was arguably the worst president in US history. I recently heard Joe Hagmann use an analogy of a corrupt police force in a corrupt city to describe what President Trump is up against. I could not agree with him more. Normally anyone who attempts to speak out against institutionalized corruption such as this ends up dead or seriously discredited prior to more extreme measures taking place. How would you respond surrounded by corruption? Can one man make a difference? Absolutely! But he needs our Prayers and Support like never before.

Most likely due to the lack of productivity from our elected officials, a good portion of the American voting population has what I call, "A Super Hero Complex" were they expect (especially their President) to come to the rescue and save them from this or that. No President should ever be treated like a Savior or superhero!

A President is a servant of the people, that simple. President Trump is not Jesus Christ nor are any presidents that have come before or will follow after him.

He is a real man that is flesh and blood and to get things done he will need to compromise in ways that make some of us that are idealist very angry. Having realistic expectations does not mean that we throw away our core principles it just means we recognize in the political system that we have compromises normally are made to bring about the best outcome for the most amount of people.

One thing to keep in mind if you're an idealist is the alternative choice that was presented to us – I can't speak for you, "But I'm Not With Her"! Does that put things in perspective for you?

What do you think your expectations would've been for "Her"? America didn't elect a choir boy America elected a bouncer to go and "Clean the Swamp". Now anyone who's ever been around long enough knows it's going to get pretty ugly before it gets pretty good – and this is why our prayer is so needed.

To truly Make America Great Again we have to stop looking for the change to come from the top down, this is never how it's been. To make America great again it's going to have to start with you and me, in fact to make America great again will require prayer and repentance before Almighty God.

Chapter 3: Doing Our Part

If you think President Donald Trump can make America great by himself alone you are sadly mistaken and haven't quite frankly them paying attention. There was an organic movement that developed in many parts of the country because people want their country back from the criminals that stole it. This grassroots movement consumed the hearts and minds of the people of the nation.

There is no way President Trump got elected by himself, the American people rose up in one accord and said enough is enough.

They stood together in harmony at rallies and speeches throughout the land and in their homes and churches praying earnestly that God would allow Donald Trump to be our next President. And God heard His people and their prayers and allowed Donald Trump to be the next President of the United States of America.

Our responsibility to stand in the gap and pray is not over. As Christians we are constantly in a war. The Bible declares the devil walks around as a roaring lion seeking whom he may devour. We have to constantly be in prayer for our nation, for our president, and for our brothers and sisters in Christ.

The enemy continues to attack and we continue to play defense – it's time to turn this situation around and go on the offensive and start tearing down the strongholds of the enemy through prayer and faith. If you're serious about taking back America, and making America Great Again then I hope that you put your righteous anger to good use during your prayer time and take authority over things in the name of Jesus Christ of Nazareth. It's up to us to be the difference and lead by example.

Remember we are a Representative Republic – "We The People"!

Chapter 4:
Why Pray for Donald Trump

Christian should not be divided over political issues but be united in one accord, in one faith, and in one Lord and Savior Jesus Christ. Having said that, the Scriptures also command us to pray for our leaders and those that exercise authority over us.

Therefore I exhort first of all that supplications, prayers, intercessions, and giving of thanks be made for all men, for kings and all who are in authority, that we may lead a quiet and peaceable life in all godliness and reverence. For this is good and acceptable in the sight of God our Savior, who desires all men to be saved and to come to the knowledge of the truth. (1 Tim 2:1-4)

For the first time in a long time we have a President that is continually asking for Prayers – whether for others or himself. The openness to ask for prayer from you and me demonstrates Presidents Trumps desire to seek the kingdom of God first and lean not unto his own understanding but in all his ways acknowledge God Almighty. Wow, we have a president who asks genuinely for prayers – what is your answer oh people of faith.

You know the Bible makes it very clear that we as God's people need to get our own house in order prior to anything else. If we want to receive the blessings of God then we have to operate in accordance and in harmony with His Word, not doing so will lead to catastrophic consequences.

The following Scripture indicates the initial plan of action for believers:

If My people who are called by My name will humble themselves, and pray and seek My face, and turn from their wicked ways, then I will hear from heaven, and will forgive their sin and heal their land. (2 Chronicles 7:14)

If we really want to Make America Great Again we will follow what the Scriptures say. Did you notice how 2 Chronicles 7:14 says, "If My People" meaning God's people. It's up to us to Humble Ourselves, Repent, and Pray and Seek God's Face if "We The People" want to be Heard and Healed – This is the Essence of Making America Great because it address the Root Problem which is Spiritual not Political.

Remember these witches are warring against president Trump, they literally are engaged in spiritual warfare against the president of the United States openly – he's under attack in the spirit. Therefore it is critical to address the threat in the spiritual realm through powerful specific fervent intercessory prayers.

What does the Scriptures say, "We do not wrestle against flesh and blood, but against principalities, against powers, against the rulers of the darkness of this age, against spiritual hosts of wickedness in the heavenly places" (Ephesians 6:12)

"The kings of the earth set themselves, and the rulers take counsel together, against the Lord and against His Anointed, saying, 'Let us break their bonds in pieces and cast away their cords from us.' He who sits in the heavens shall laugh ..." (Psalm 2:2-4)

We have the ultimate victory in Christ. However, our nation and the entire free world's "Fate" depend on America becoming great again and this hinges on the faith action of believers right now – Will You Pray? If America falls, the entire world will be plunged into a new dark age, your prayers are needed now like never before. So let's learn more in the following chapters about what prayer really is and how we can fight back against the evil of the day

Chapter 5: What is Prayer

Prayer is conversation between you and God. It is both speaking and listening. You speak. God listens. God speaks. You listen.

You speak

Prayer is the time you spend talking to God about the cares and concerns of your heart. It is the time you tell Him the desires of your heart. It is time spent praising God for being His amazing, holy, and wonderful self. It is time spent confessing your sins and asking God's forgiveness. It is time spent talking to God on behalf of family, friends, your church, our government, our military, missionaries, and whoever or whatever else concerns you.

God listens

God listens to each and every word we say. He even listens to our thoughts. Philippians 4:6 says, *Be careful for nothing; but in every thing by prayer and supplication with thanksgiving let your requests be made known unto God.* Did you get that? We can (and should) go to God about everything.

God listened to Elijah when he questioned God's decision to allow the widow's son to die. Once more, God gave Elijah what he asked for: *And he cried unto the Lord, and said, O Lord my God, hast thou also brought evil upon the widow with whom I sojourn, by slaying her son? And he stretched himself upon the child three times, and cried unto the Lord, and said, O Lord my God, I pray thee, let this child's soul come into him again.*

And the Lord heard the voice of Elijah; and the soul of the child came into him again, and he revived. (1ˢᵗ Kings 17:20-22)

God listened to Mordecai when he prayed that God would intervene and save the Jewish race from annihilation at the hand of Haman (Esther4:1).

God listened to David when he asked God to forgive him for his sins of adultery and conspiracy for murder. David's prayer asking forgiveness is one of the most beautiful of all the psalms...

Have mercy upon me, O God, according to thy lovingkindness: according unto the multitude of thy tender mercies blot out my transgressions.

Wash me throughly from mine iniquity, and cleanse me from my sin. For I acknowledge my transgressions: and my sin is ever before me. Against thee, thee only, have I sinned, and done this evil in thy sight: that thou mightest be justified when thou speakest, and be clear when thou judgest... Purge me with hyssop, and I shall be clean: wash me, and I shall be whiter than snow. Make me to hear joy and gladness; that the bones which thou hast broken may rejoice. Hide thy face from my sins, and blot out all mine iniquities. Create in me a clean heart, O God; and renew a right spirit within me. Cast me not away from thy presence; and take not thy holy spirit from me. Restore unto me the joy of thy salvation; and uphold me with thy free spirit. (Psalm 51:1-4 and 7-12)

God listened to Jesus when He asked God to forgive those who were responsible for His death when He said, *"Then said Jesus, Father, forgive them; for they know not what they do." (Luke 23:34)*

God speaks

When we pray, we're not the only ones doing the talking. God does plenty of talking when we pray. No, we don't audibly hear God's voice like Abraham, Moses, Jonah, and numerous others did normally. But we hear God in that little voice that speaks to our heart and to our mind; telling us to do what we know is right and good. God's voice is the voice that warns us against sin and encourages us to go in the direction He created us to go.

Abraham's servant prayed to God; asking Him to provide the right woman for him to take home for Isaac to marry...

And he said O Lord God of my master Abraham, I pray thee, send me good speed this day, and shew kindness unto my master Abraham. Behold, I stand here by the well of water; and the daughters of the men of the city come out to draw water: And let it come to pass, that the damsel to whom I shall say,

Let down thy pitcher, I pray thee, that I may drink; and she shall say, Drink, and I will give thy camels drink also: let the same be she that thou hast appointed for thy servant Isaac; and thereby shall I know that thou hast shewed kindness unto my master. (Genesis 24:12-14)

God spoke to this man by giving him exactly what he asked for—a clear and definite answer as to the girl he was to take home to Isaac.

God audibly spoke to Moses countless times. One that especially stands out in my mind was the time God was so angry at the Israelites for building the golden calf and worshipping it that He told Moses He was going to kill them all and start over—creating a nation of people from Moses rather than Abraham. Let's look at this incident and then talk about it some more...

And the Lord said unto Moses, Go, get thee down; for thy people, which thou broughtest out of the land of Egypt, have corrupted themselves:

They have turned aside quickly out of the way which I commanded them: they have made them a molten calf, and have worshipped it, and have sacrificed thereunto, and said, These be thy gods, O Israel, which have brought thee up out of the land of Egypt. And the Lord said unto Moses, I have seen this people, and, behold, it is a stiffnecked people: Now therefore let me alone, that my wrath may wax hot against them, and that I may consume them: and I will make of thee a great nation. And Moses besought the Lord his God, and said, Lord, why doth thy wrath wax hot against thy people, which thou hast brought forth out of the land of Egypt with great power, and with a mighty hand? Wherefore should the Egyptians speak, and say, For mischief did he bring them out, to slay them in the mountains, and to consume them from the face of the earth?

Turn from thy fierce wrath, and repent of this evil against thy people. Remember Abraham, Isaac, and Israel, thy servants, to whom thou swarest by thine own self, and saidst unto them, I will multiply your seed as the stars of heaven, and all this land that I have spoken of will I give unto your seed, and they shall inherit it for ever. And the Lord repented of the evil which he thought to do unto his people. (Exodus 2:7-14)

Some might say this wasn't actually a prayer, but considering the fact that prayer is conversation between us and God, I'd say it most definitely was.

Keeping that in mind, let's take a more in-depth look at what God was *saying* to Moses in this brief encounter:

God is instructing Moses; telling him to go down to the people.

God is voicing his anger and hurt because Israel was so quick to turn their backs on God.

It would have been or at least tempting (to some degree) for Moses to say, "Go ahead! Wipe them out and make me the new root of your people." But Moses didn't do that. Moses once again proved himself to be the humble servant of God he was. He reminded God of the promise He made to Abraham and telling God that he was trusting in Him to keep that promise.

God voiced his pleasure with Moses in being so faithful and humble. He then did just what He had promised Abraham and allowed the Israelites to live.

God spoke to Paul when He didn't give Paul what he asked for—to take away whatever chronic ailment (thorn in the flesh) Paul was dealing with.

He wanted Paul to understand that he could be just as effective (if not more so) in the ministry with the ailment as he could without it. God wanted Paul to remember that the work he was doing was *through* him (Paul) *by* God.

FYI: God wants us to know the same.

You listen

The listening part of prayer on our part can be summed up in one word. Obedience.

Jonah didn't listen to God and paid a pretty steep price for his disobedience (Jonah 1). In spite of Jonah's disobedience God still listened to Jonah and gave him another chance.

Ezekiel obeyed God; leading him to have to do some incredibly awkward, humiliating, and 'interesting' things.

Jesus listened to God throughout His life and ministry here on earth, but never so obviously as He did the night He was arrested. Prior to His arrest, Jesus prayed; asking if there was any other way to bring about salvation for you and me. God said no, and Jesus' reply was "Your will be done".

The act of prayer is an act of communication, but it is also what we call a spiritual discipline. The term itself is not found in the Bible, but is one the Church uses to define those things necessary to become more mature and solid in your relationship with God. They are things we need to make part of our character and normal daily lives. You can see by the definition that prayer most certainly falls into that category.

Chapter 6: How Do We Pray

Jesus out and out told us how we should pray in the Sermon on the Mount (Matthew 5-7). We refer to this instruction in how to pray as the Lord's Prayer. His instruction is primarily what to pray *for* or *about* rather than actually how to pray, so we're going to save that passage of scripture for another chapter. Instead, we're going to look at how to pray as in what our attitude and approach to prayer should be.

Approaching God in Faith

Let's look at a few verses in the Bible on the subject of approaching God in prayer in faith. In doing so we will discover that faith is the key to hearing and receiving God's answers to our prayers.

*Therefore I say unto you, What things
soever ye desire, when ye pray, believe that
ye receive them, and ye shall have them.*
~Mark 11:24

This one (and similar verses) are most likely
the most misunderstood verse in the Bible.
If not, it definitely rates in the top three.
Why? Because it is taken out of context,
that's why. If you read the verses just prior
to this, you will find that Jesus is speaking to
the disciples about faith. He tells them that
if they have a strong enough faith they can
do anything in His name. He then tells them
that whatever they ask for they can have, as
well. But this is what is called an implied
statement. Jesus is implying (not specifically
mentioning because the suggestion or
understanding is already there) that they
wouldn't ask for anything outside the
perimeters of one living a faithful, obedient
life.

In other words, you wouldn't ask for things that would draw your heart, soul, and mind away from the Father or the Son. You would ask for things (material and otherwise) that would be of physical, emotional, and spiritual benefit to you and to others.

And this is the confidence that we have in him, that, if we ask any thing according to his will, he heareth us: and if we know that he hear us, whatsoever we ask, we know that we have the petitions that we desired of him. `1ˢᵗ John 5:14-15

If ye abide in me, and my words abide in you, ye shall ask what ye will, and it shall be done unto you. ~John 15:7

And all things, whatsoever ye shall ask in prayer, believing, ye shall receive. ~Matthew 21:22

Both of these verses are also on the end of Jesus' comments about the need for faith and being one with Him—heart, soul, and mind.

But let him ask in faith, nothing wavering. For he that wavereth is like a wave of the sea driven with the wind and tossed. For let not that man think that he shall receive any thing of the Lord. A double minded man is unstable in all his ways. ~James 1:6-8

Praying without having faith is like stopping at all the green lights because you don't have faith they will stay green long enough for you to make it through the intersection.

But without faith it is impossible to please him: for he that cometh to God must believe that he is, and that he is a rewarder of them that diligently seek him. ~Hebrews 11:6

This is one of the most beautiful yet telling verses in the Bible. God promises to reward anyone who diligently seeks Him, but reminds us that this is not possible unless we have a faith that is rock-solid. He knows there will be times when we question whether

He is listening because we aren't getting the results we want when we want them. The faith He is talking about here is the faith that never loses sight of the fact that God is real, holy, almighty – and ultimately in control.

Pray Persistently

Pray without ceasing. ~1st Thessalonians 5:17

Call unto me, and I will answer thee, and show thee great and mighty things, which thou knowest not. ~Jeremiah 33:3

Keep asking. Keep talking. Keep listening. God will answer by giving you the promptings of the Holy Spirit, through the works and encouragement of others, and through the events in your life that too many people chalk up to coincidence, happenstance, and fate.

And he spake a parable unto them to this end, that men ought always to pray, and not to faint; Saying, There was in a city a judge, which feared not God, neither regarded man: And there was a widow in that city; and she came unto him, saying, Avenge me of mine adversary. And he would not for a while: but afterward he said within himself, Though I fear not God, nor regard man; yet because this widow troubleth me, I will avenge her, lest by her continual coming she weary me. And the Lord said, Hear what the unjust judge saith. And shall not God avenge his own elect, which cry day and night unto him, though he bear long with them? I tell you that he will avenge them speedily. Nevertheless when the Son of man cometh, shall he find faith on the earth? ~Luke 18:1-18

Jesus' parable is a reminder that God often wants or needs to know how serious or determined we are for what we pray for. Are we genuinely ready for whatever? Are we resolved to handle His answer?

Pray in Agreement with God

Delight thyself also in the Lord: and he shall give thee the desires of thine heart. ~Psalm 37:4

When we are living obediently and faithfully to God, He will give us the desires of our heart because the first desire of our heart will be to do God's will and those that follow will be in line with what God created us to do and be.

Confess your faults one to another, and pray one for another, that ye may be healed. The effectual fervent prayer of a righteous man availeth much. ~James 5:16

For if ye forgive men their trespasses, your heavenly Father will also forgive you: But if ye forgive not men their trespasses, neither will your Father forgive your trespasses. ~Matthew 6:14-15

God cannot and will not answer the prayers of those who refuse to confess their sins to Him or those who refuse to forgive those who have sinned against them.

If my people, which are called by my name, shall humble themselves, and pray, and seek my face, and turn from their wicked ways; then will I hear from heaven, and will forgive their sin, and will heal their land.
~2nd Chronicles 7:14

We must be willing to humble ourselves to the authority and sovereignty of God. We must acknowledge God as the giver of all *because it is all His to give.*

Pray Expecting Answers

My voice shalt thou hear in the morning, O Lord; in the morning will I direct my prayer unto thee, and will look up. ~Psalm 5:3

David looked up because he knew God was going to answer him. He just knew. I love that because it just shows how sure David was of his God. We should be just as sure today.

Be careful for nothing; but in every thing by prayer and supplication with thanksgiving let your requests be made known unto God. And the peace of God, which passeth all understanding, shall keep your hearts and minds through Christ Jesus. ~Philippians 4:6-7

He shall call upon me, and I will answer him: I will be with him in trouble; I will deliver him, and honour him. ~Psalm 91:15

The promise of God should be enough to let us know that our prayers will be answered. It is important to remember, though, that answered prayer isn't always answered the way we want or think it should be.

No parent always tells their child yes, so why should God be any different? He is the God of the 'big picture'. He knows what is going to be and what is best for us in the days, weeks, and years ahead.

But they that wait upon the Lord shall renew their strength; they shall mount up with wings as eagles; they shall run, and not be weary; and they shall walk, and not faint.
~Isaiah 40:31

God's timing is always the perfect timing. We need to remember this—to not get tired of waiting and to not refuse the strength and comfort He offers while we wait. We must also be mindful of not refusing to see God's answer to our prayer if it differs from what we think it should be.

If not, hearken unto me: hold thy peace, and I shall teach thee wisdom. ~Job 33:33

This verse from Job reminds us that in order for God to answer our prayers we have to be quiet long enough to hear Him. Job wanted answers but was too busy telling God he wanted them to hear God speaking. But God got Job's attention—just like He will get ours.

In faith, with persistence and expectation and a heart that longs to be right with God—this is the 'recipe' for how to pray.

Chapter 7:
Does Prayer Work

We know what Prayer is and kind of How to Pray . . . But Why Pray? Answering the Why is to understand the motivation behind your actions let me start out by asking this, why do you talk to your best friend, your spouse, your employer, or other people around you? Now sometimes you may not want to talk to your spouse, your employer or even your best friend because of whatever issues that are between you or maybe because you know you're in trouble with your employer.

The fact remains, however, despite whatever the circumstances are in our daily life between these individuals we have to communicate and interact with them just about every day. Why should it be any different with your relationship with God – the one that created you and gave you life?

The short answer is it should not be any different, well let me back up, it should be different if you truly know who God is. So that's the question, who is God to you? When you answer this question you're going to be one step closer to answering a very personal question, why pray? Now sure there are basic reasons why we should all pray but it really boils down to your relationship with God and who God is to you. The more that you read His Word, the more that you spend time with God in prayer, the more that you draw close to Him the more the God will mean to you.

Recently Valentine's Day had just passed, now I'm not a fan of this particular holiday if that's what you want to call it because I feel that you should be showing your love each and every day to the person that you're with.

Nevertheless it brings me to a point to help you better understand something here.

For those that are married do you remember falling in love with your spouse? Do you remember what it was like to have that all-consuming desire and love for them? Do you remember how you couldn't wait until you were able to see them again or talk with them again? We need to have a love relationship with Jesus Christ in a similar fashion. Now I am not talking about a romantic love but a passionate love nonetheless that seeks to have a servant's heart and a sincere desire to do God's will.

Interesting enough if we look at couples that have been married for a long period of time often times you will find the spark has died, they may barely see each other because of work, and hardly ever speak except for talking about the necessities of life such as bills and the kids. This is a great example of how most of our prayer lives are with God.

We have to get back that spark – do you remember when you first came to the Lord how passionate and on fire you were to serve Him and to pray and communicate with him?

Brothers and sisters it's time for a revival within each of us and then collectively as we organically come together in the spirit – let's start a resurrection and a revival once again, and let it start right now within each of us. And then you will understand why you need to pray.

Continuing on with the relationship theme, how many marriages end in divorce because of adultery, abuse or neglect? How many of us have a prayer life that is in similar disarray?

If you're not praying to God but you're sitting in front of the television for hours each day or listening to music is this not adultery if you do not make equal time for God?

Are you abusing your relationship with God by only coming to Him in prayer when you need or want something? Are you neglecting your relationship with Almighty God potentially because of sin that is crêpe in and now hold you captive?

Let me explain how the pattern works brothers and sisters first it starts with neglect then it leads to abuse and ultimately adultery or idolatry as the Bible describes it. It's a vicious cycle but one that can be broken with the blood of the lamb, one that can be broken through committing yourself to learning and getting close to God both in His Word and in Prayer.

Why Pray? Well here's some basic answers:

- Because You Love God
- To Keep Your Relationship with God Strong
- Because You love your family, friends, country etc
- Because you want to see God's will done on Earth as it is in heaven
- To Fight Back Against your Spiritual Enemy
- To Walk in the Authority God has Given You

Remember, prayer is a tangible real thing that should not be discarded or put to the side until you have an emergency or crisis. Is that the kind of relationship you want someone to have with you?

Learn to have a good relationship with God by talking with Him daily in prayer.

So many of us continue to struggle and have such a poor prayer life because we don't recognize prayer for what it truly is and just how powerful it is. It should not be your last resort – it should be your immediate response to situations, circumstances, and dealing with our spiritual enemy's attacks.

You must learn to see these attacks for what they are and address them accordingly in prayer – taking authority over the enemy in the name of Jesus. How many of us understand and recognize that every single day of our lives we are in a spiritual war and that prayer is essential for living a victorious life in Christ? How much more so is President Trump – Now is the time to Pray!

Chapter 8: Make Prayer a Priority

Unfortunately many Christians do not make prayer a priority. They get swept away with the cares of this life, paying the bills, tending to the kids, or dealing with the crazy dog – life happens and it seems to happen so quickly.

Making time to pray requires self-discipline that is also in short supply in a fast food nation. The true prayer warriors are few and far between yet their number bears no regard to the effectiveness of their prayers. It's time for the people of God to get serious about their prayer lives because if you don't have a strong prayer life you don't have a strong relationship with Jesus Christ.

Making time to pray is one of the biggest complaints and hurdles Christians say they are faced with. I get it—life is hectic. We have all sorts of people and things vying for our time and attention. It only seems practical or reasonable to put the things that are staring us in the face first. But oh, what a mistake that is!

To help put it into perspective, let me ask you the following questions:

- Would you consider eating dinner and going to bed instead of picking your child up from sports practice or piano lessons because you are at home and able to *see* dinner cooking on the stove and your bedroom, but cannot see your child while they are at practice/lessons?
- Would you consider not paying your insurance premiums in order to buy new furniture because you can see the furniture but not the benefits of having the insurance?

- Would you not call your parents or grandparents to talk with them or check on their well-being if seeing them on a regular basis was not possible? You know, the 'out of sight, out of mind' philosophy?

I am hoping and praying you answered each of these questions with an emphatic NO. Why, then, do you relegate God and prayer to a status of 'bottom of the totem pole' (last place)?

Whether or not you make time to pray shouldn't be the question. The question should be what you have time for *after* you pray. You might have to give up a television show, a few less minutes in the book you are reading, one less round of golf, or take one less class at the gym, but prayer should take precedence over the activities in your life.

How to make time to pray

If your response to the last statement is something resembling denial that you are too busy or that you cannot possibly give up *that,* you seriously need to re-think your priorities.

That being said, I don't want you to feel that what you do with your day is of no importance or significance. That is why I want to offer you the following suggestions on how to make time to pray:

- Set aside a special time for prayer each day. A time of completely being focused on conversing with God is essential in your relationship with Him. Think about it: you wouldn't appreciate it if your spouse or your children never took the time to focus on talking to you.

You would feel slighted and unimportant. You would feel you were in the way and an inconvenient duty rather than a treasured and cherished loved one.

This is exactly how God feels when we fit Him in when we have a minute here and there or if we are in over our heads and need His divine intervention. By taking the time to be solely focused on prayer each day, you will know God so much more intimately; making it possible for you to avoid many of the issues people use to distance themselves from seeking God's face each day.

- Pray before all Meals and as a Family
- Pray before you drive anywhere and Pray as you are driving: hands on the wheel, eyes on the road, pray for safety, pray for those you meet on the road, pray for the ability to be a witness of God's goodness in all you do and say throughout your day.
- Pray while fixing your kids' breakfast or lunch. Pray for their safety, that they will make right choices, and that they will seek to have a personal relationship with God each and every day of their lives.
- Pray while taking a walk. Pray for your community, your church, our government and military, and for those you know who have specific needs.

- Pray when you first open your eyes each morning. Thank God for the rest you enjoyed, for His amazing grace, for the fact that He is God, and for the precious gift of salvation.
- Pray when you lay your head on the pillow at night. When you make conversation and thoughts of God among the last ones you have each night, you can go to sleep with the peace that passes all understanding.

FYI: Often time's people say they feel guilty falling asleep at night in the middle of their prayers. But I will share with you something I read a while back on that very subject: nothing could be sweeter than drifting off to sleep while talking with your creator. What better company could you possibly have?

Again, I know it isn't always easy to push the hustle and bustle of life out of the way, but for anyone who claims Jesus as Savior, it is something you simply must do in order to make your words more than just lip service. Making prayer a priority is also worth it - Always worth it.

To give you a bit of encouragement and inspiration take a few minutes to read through the following Bible verses. I also encourage and challenge you to commit at least two or three of them to memory so that they can serve as your reminders each and every day.

Pray without ceasing. ~1st Thessalonians 5:17

Any time is a good time to pray. Prayer can be a few words spoken out loud or mentally spoken. Prayer can be a cry for help, a shout of praise, a desperate plea, or a heart to heart conversation that lasts as long as it needs to last.

Likewise the Spirit also helpeth our infirmities: for we know not what we should pray for as we ought: but the Spirit itself maketh intercession for us with groanings which cannot be uttered. ~Romans 8:26

I know someone whose prayer is simply this: "LORD, I know You know what is best and that all things work out for Your good, so please just give me the faith, courage, and strength to hold on for the ride."

But thou, when thou prayest, enter into thy closet, and when thou hast shut thy door, pray to thy Father which is in secret; and thy Father which seeth in secret shall reward thee openly. ~Matthew 6:6

This is the time we spend in focused, personal prayer.

What is it then? I will pray with the spirit, and I will pray with the understanding also: I will sing with the spirit, and I will sing with the understanding also. ~1st Corinthians 14:15

Prayers can also be songs, short and simple words of praise, and thank-you for God's protection, comfort, and active presence in situations.

Praying always with all prayer and supplication in the Spirit, and watching thereunto with all perseverance and supplication for all saints ~Ephesians 6:18

As for me, I will call upon God; and the Lord shall save me. Evening, and morning, and at noon, will I pray, and cry aloud: and he shall hear my voice. ~Psalm 55:16-17

Again...there's never a bad time to pray.

Chapter 9:
Developing a Prayer Wall

In this chapter we are going to discuss developing and building a prayer wall for President Donald Trump. It seems only fitting to build a prayer wall for President Trump since he is in fact trying to build a wall to help protect us as well. But first let's try to wrap our head around the concept of a prayer wall – what exactly is a prayer wall to begin with?

A prayer wall could be considered a lot of different things to a lot of different people depending upon the country that therein and the religion that they practice. However, what I am specifically talking about is a Christian prayer wall. A Christian prayer wall is spiritual in nature. In the spirit it literally is a wall of protection that is manifested through your faithful fervent prayers.

To further clarify we need to build a Christian prayer wall that covers President Donald Trump 24/7, 365 Days a Year. This Christian prayer wall should be comprised of faithful men and women of God who have been called to be prayer warriors and interceders for those around them.

If each and every Christian out there dedicated 15 minutes, 30 minutes, 1 hour, or whatever the Lord puts on your heart we would be able to pray for president trump 24 hours a day, seven days a week, 365 days a year – and this is our goal.

I encourage every single person who is reading this book to prayerfully consider dedicating time each day to pray for president trump and our nation. Then to please email me the specific time that you have devoted to praying each day so I can start to develop an accurate time frame as to when prayer is still needed for President.

If you live outside of the United States but still understand how important it is to pray for the President of the United States you are more than welcome to join this Christian prayer wall. Furthermore, it doesn't matter what denomination you are, if you believe on the Lord Jesus Christ and the power of prayer we want you to be a part of this.

Again please drop us an email on our website listed at the end of this book as to when you will be praying, your location, and your name. If you do not want us to use your name on our website please let us know that in advance and we will simply use your initials. If anyone reading this book knows of an active Christian prayer wall already in existence praying specifically for and interceding on behalf of president trump please also let me know that as well when you contact us.

We should not be in competition with one another but cooperating with one another in a spirit of love and compassion for our brothers and sisters worldwide.

Now that we've established a general concept and understanding of the Christian prayer wall that we are trying to develop to cover and protect President Donald Trump we need to look at what to pray for next. It's important to have at least some specific things that we are praying for altogether and from there move as the Spirit leads. But remember what the Scripture says . . . .

"Again I say to you that if two of you agree on earth concerning anything that they ask, it will be done for them by My Father in heaven. (Matthew 18:19)

Things to Pray:

- Plead the Blood of Jesus over President Donald Trump, his family, his advisers, those that voted for him, and those that support him as a hedge of protection against the enemy.
- Bind and rebuke any and all that are coming up against them in the spirit in the name of Jesus Christ of Nazareth
- Pray that God's perfect and holy will would be done in each of their lives
- Pray for the salvation of each of them (if they are not already saved)
- Pray that President Trump does not lean on to his own understanding but in all of his ways acknowledges God Almighty
- Pray that president trump seeks the kingdom of God first and his righteousness

- Pray that God leads him, and guides him, and protects him against all enemies foreign or domestic, spiritual or physical, seen or unseen, whether he's awake or whether he's asleep
- Pray that God protects them from himself and from the Council of fools
- Pray that God would give him wisdom to faithfully lead this nation and to honor God and all that he does
- Pray that President Trump would walk in integrity before the Lord our God all the days of his life
- Pray that the Fear of the Lord would be ever upon him for it is the beginning of wisdom
- Pray that President Trump would be surrounded by godly advisors
- Pray that President Trump would receive critical information, truth, and revelations
- Pray that President Trump would seek justice for the American people

that the name of our Lord God
would be glorified here on earth.
- Pray that President Trump will
  safeguard and protect the innocent
  and those that are most vulnerable
  in our society.

This is just the starting point of our focused
Christian prayer wall for President Donald
Trump. If you think of other things to add to
this list please send me an email so I can
either add it within this book or on the
website. Again this Christian prayer wall
should be interactive, Christians
everywhere should be rising up in prayer for
the present United States, coming together
in one accord, in one spirit and in one Lord
and Savior Jesus Christ.

Chapter 10:
Learning to Pray Stronger

If you're going to help make America great again through prayer it's important to learn how to be a prayer warrior. A prayer warrior—sounds a little intimidating, doesn't it? Don't worry, though. It's not. A prayer warrior is merely a term used to describe someone who is vigilant and ceaseless in their prayers.

A prayer warrior is someone who knows and counts on the power of prayer to bring about change and blessing in their life and the lives of others. A Prayer Warrior is someone who understands there is a Spiritual War going on all the time. They intercede for themselves and others by binding, rebuking, and taking authority over the enemy through faith and prayer.

A prayer warrior is someone who understands the power of prayer and the authority Christ has given us and operates in faith and courage to do battle against spiritual forces of darkness.

There are several methods people use to help them establish a strong and consistent prayer life. We're going to look at a few of them now in an effort to help you do the same.

Pray without ceasing

Pray without ceasing. ~1st Thessalonians 5:17 Your mom always told you that practice makes perfect when it came time to practice your music lessons, or learn your multiplication facts. Well, the same holds true for the discipline of prayer. Practice makes perfect.

The more you pray the more you will want to pray and the more you want to pray the more reliant you will become on God. And that, my friend, is about as perfect as it gets this side of heaven.

ACTS Acronym

Adoration: Giving God the glory, praise and honor due Him. Praising God for creation and for His forever-ness.

> *Who being the brightness of his glory, and the express image of his person, and upholding all things by the word of his power, when he had by himself purged our sins, sat down on the right hand of the Majesty on high: ~Hebrews 1:3*

And every creature which is in heaven, and on the earth, and under the earth, and such as are in the sea, and all that are in them, heard I saying, Blessing, and honour, and glory, and power, be unto him that sitteth upon the throne, and unto the Lamb for ever and ever.
~Revelation 5:13

And thou shalt love the Lord thy God with all thy heart, and with all thy soul, and with all thy mind, and with all thy strength: this is the first commandment.
~Mark 12:30

Praise ye the Lord. Praise God in his sanctuary: praise him in the firmament of his power. Praise him for his mighty acts: praise him according to his excellent greatness. Praise him with the sound of the trumpet: praise him with the psaltery and harp. Praise him with the timbrel and dance: praise him with stringed instruments and organs. Praise him upon the loud cymbals: praise him upon the high sounding cymbals. Let every thing that hath breath praise the Lord. Praise ye the Lord. ~Psalm 150

Confession: Confessing your sins to God specifically, humbly, and with a heart of true repentance.

If we confess our sins, he is faithful and just to forgive us our sins, and to cleanse us from all unrighteousness. ~1st John 1:9

He that covereth his sins shall not prosper: but whoso confesseth and forsaketh them shall have mercy. ~Proverbs 28:13

Submit yourselves therefore to God. Resist the devil, and he will flee from you. Draw nigh to God, and he will draw nigh to you. Cleanse your hands, ye sinners; and purify your hearts, ye double minded. Be afflicted, and mourn, and weep: let your laughter be turned to mourning, and your joy to heaviness. Humble yourselves in the sight of the Lord, and he shall lift you up. ~James 4:7-10

Have mercy upon me, O God, according to thy lovingkindness: according unto the multitude of thy tender mercies blot out my transgressions. Wash me throughly from mine iniquity, and cleanse me from my sin. For I acknowledge my transgressions: and my sin is ever before me. ~Psalm 51:1-3

Thanksgiving: Give thanks to God for His blessings, His love, His mercy, His gift of salvation, and for the hope of heaven.

Giving thanks always for all things unto God and the Father in the name of our Lord Jesus Christ; ~Ephesians 5:20

O give thanks unto the God of heaven: for his mercy endureth for ever. ~Psalm 136:26

Bless the Lord, O my soul, and forget not all his benefits... ~Psalm 103:2

Enter into his gates with thanksgiving,
and into his courts with praise: be
thankful unto him, and bless his name.
~Psalm 100:4

Supplication: Praying on behalf of others and asking for the things we need and desire is definitely a part of prayer. Remember: prayer is communicating with God for the purpose of developing a deeper relationship with Him. That cannot happen if we aren't honest with God and if we don't open ourselves up completely to Him.

And this is the confidence that we have
in him, that, if we ask any thing
according to his will, he heareth us... ~1st
John 5:14

Ye ask, and receive not, because ye ask
amiss, that ye may consume it upon
your lusts. ~James 4:3

But let him ask in faith, nothing wavering. For he that wavereth is like a wave of the sea driven with the wind and tossed. For let not that man think that he shall receive any thing of the Lord. A double minded man is unstable in all his ways. ~James 1:6-8

My help cometh from the Lord, which made heaven and earth. ~Psalm 121:2

Come unto me, all ye that labour and are heavy laden, and I will give you rest. ~Matthew 11:28

And the Lord turned the captivity of Job, when he prayed for his friends: also the Lord gave Job twice as much as he had before. ~Job 42:10

PRAY Acronym

The PRAY acronym is another often-used method of developing good prayer habits. As you can see, it is quite similar to the ACTS acronym, but then why wouldn't it be? They all follow the model prayer (the LORD's prayer) in Matthew 6.

There is, however, one aspect of the PRAY acronym I think needs to be highlighted. It is the Y, which reminds us to yield to God's purpose for our lives. So while I won't take the time to repeat every scripture used above for the ACTS acronym, I will insert a few of them in the appropriate place then focus on some that deal with yielding to God's will.

Praise: Giving God the glory, praise and honor due Him. Praising God for creation and for His forever-ness.

Who being the brightness of his glory, and the express image of his person, and upholding all things by the word of his power, when he had by himself purged our sins, sat down on the right hand of the Majesty on high: ~Hebrews 1:3

And every creature which is in heaven, and on the earth, and under the earth, and such as are in the sea, and all that are in them, heard I saying, Blessing, and honour, and glory, and power, be unto him that sitteth upon the throne, and unto the Lamb for ever and ever. ~Revelation 5:13

Repent: To repent means to change your ways. It is a reversing of yourself from living a sinful lifestyle to a Godly lifestyle.

And the times of this ignorance God winked at; but now commandeth all men every where to repent... Acts 17:30

Know ye not that the unrighteous shall not inherit the kingdom of God? Be not deceived: neither fornicators, nor idolaters, nor adulterers, nor effeminate, nor abusers of themselves with mankind, nor thieves, nor covetous, nor drunkards, nor revilers, nor extortioners, shall inherit the kingdom of God. ~1st Corinthians 6:9-10

Then Peter said unto them, Repent, and be baptized every one of you in the name of Jesus Christ for the remission of sins, and ye shall receive the gift of the Holy Ghost. ~Acts 2:38

And be not conformed to this world: but be ye transformed by the renewing of your mind, that ye may prove what is that good, and acceptable, and perfect, will of God. ~Romans 12:2

And fear not them which kill the body, but are not able to kill the soul: but rather fear him which is able to destroy both soul and body in hell. ~Matthew 10:28

Ask: Asking God for the desires of your heart, for the needs you have in your life, and for the provision and safety for others all comes under this 'category'.

Ye ask, and receive not, because ye ask amiss, that ye may consume it upon your lusts. ~James 4:3

But let him ask in faith, nothing wavering. For he that wavereth is like a wave of the sea driven with the wind and tossed. For let not that man think that he shall receive any thing of the Lord. A double minded man is unstable in all his ways. ~James 1:6-8

My help cometh from the Lord, which made heaven and earth. ~Psalm 121:2

Come unto me, all ye that labour and are heavy laden, and I will give you rest. ~Matthew 11:28

Yield: To yield is to give in—to allow God to have His way in your life. Yielding is submission and obedience. Yielding is also living by faith.

For God so loved the world, that he gave his only begotten Son, that whosoever believeth in him should not perish, but have everlasting life. ~John 3:16

What? know ye not that your body is the temple of the Holy Ghost which is in you, which ye have of God, and ye are not your own? ~1st Corinthians 6:19

Trust in the Lord with all thine heart; and lean not unto thine own understanding. In all thy ways acknowledge him, and he shall direct thy paths. Be not wise in thine own eyes: fear the Lord, and depart from evil. ~Proverbs 3:5-7

But be ye doers of the word, and not hearers only, deceiving your own selves. For if any be a hearer of the word, and not a doer, he is like unto a man beholding his natural face in a glass: For he beholdeth himself, and goeth his way, and straightway forgetteth what manner of man he was. But whoso looketh into the perfect law of liberty, and continueth therein, he being not a forgetful hearer, but a doer of the work, this man shall be blessed in his deed. ~James 1:22-25

Be ye therefore followers of God, as dear children. ~Ephesians 5:1

For if we sin wilfully after that we have received the knowledge of the truth, there remaineth no more sacrifice for sins, But a certain fearful looking for of judgment and fiery indignation, which shall devour the adversaries. ~Hebrews 10:26-27

God is a Spirit: and they that worship him must worship him in spirit and in truth. ~John 4:24

I'll say it again: a prayer warrior is someone who understands, believes in, and depends on the power of prayer. Be a prayer warrior and help Make America Great Again by praying for President Trump and his big agenda.

Chapter 11:
Praying and Spiritual Warfare

By now you should have some understanding as to what spiritual warfare is. However, for those that do not we will do our best to help you understand. Spiritual Warfare may sound even scarier and more intimidating than the term 'Prayer Warrior'. That's because it can actually be a very scary thing if you don't know what you're doing or who you are in Christ Jesus. Learn from the clear example below in the Word of God not to try this unless you know who you are in Christ.

Acts 19:11-17

Now God worked unusual miracles by the hands of Paul, so that even handkerchiefs or aprons were brought from his body to the sick, and the diseases left them and the evil spirits went out of them. Then some of the itinerant Jewish exorcists took it upon themselves to call the name of the Lord Jesus over those who had evil spirits, saying, "We exorcise you by the Jesus whom Paul preaches." Also there were seven sons of Sceva, a Jewish chief priest, who did so. And the evil spirit answered and said, "Jesus I know, and Paul I know; but who are you?" Then the man in whom the evil spirit was leaped on them, overpowered them, and prevailed against them, so that they fled out of that house naked and wounded. This became known both to all Jews and Greeks dwelling in Ephesus; and fear fell on them all, and the name of the Lord Jesus was magnified.

Now I'm not trying to scare you here but you have to understand there is a real war going on between the Kingdom of God and the kingdom of the devil. This is a spiritual war with earthly consequences. Fallen Angels, demons, and demonic possession are all very real things and is not something that the novice should get into with little to no training. One of the best men of God in our age to learn this from is Russ Dizdar. His website is www.shatterthedarkness.com for those interested in learning more about his ministry.

We don't need to be scared of the devil but mindful of his ways and unrelenting attacks on our hearts, souls, minds, and bodies.

Be sober, be vigilant; because your adversary the devil walks about like a roaring lion, seeking whom he may devour. Resist him, steadfast in the faith, knowing that the same sufferings are experienced by your brotherhood in the world – (1 Peter 5:8-9)

Lest Satan should take advantage of us; for we are not ignorant of his devices – (2 Cor. 2:11)

Therefore submit to God. Resist the devil and he will flee from you. – (James 4:7)

We don't need to be afraid of what the devil can do to us, we have been given authority over him and all his evil minions. We don't need to even be afraid of being separated from God somehow either here on earth or for all eternity. Let's let the Scriptures speak for themselves, below you can see that nothing can separate us from the love of God in Christ Jesus in addition to Christ giving us all authority to trample on serpents and scorpions and over all the power of the enemy – did you see the word all. That sounds pretty absolute to me.

The main thing that we need to realize here is what manner of spirit we are of – 2 Tim 1:7 makes it very clear that God has not given us a spirit of fear, but of power, and of love, and of a sound mind.

For I am persuaded that neither death nor life, nor angels nor principalities nor powers, nor things present nor things to come, nor height nor depth, nor any other created thing, shall be able to separate us from the love of God which is in Christ Jesus our Lord –(Rom. 8:38-39)

You are of God, little children, and have overcome them, because He who is in you is greater than he who is in the world –(1 John 4:4)

Then the seventy returned with joy, saying, "Lord, even the demons are subject to us in Your name." And He said to them, "I saw Satan fall like lightning from heaven. Behold, I give you the authority to trample on serpents and scorpions, and over all the power of the enemy, and nothing shall by any means hurt you. Nevertheless do not rejoice in this, that the spirits are subject to you, but rather rejoice because your names are written in heaven – (Luke 10: 17-20)

For God has not given us a spirit of fear, but of power and of love and of a sound mind – (2 Tim 1:7)

There is no fear in love; but perfect love casts out fear, because fear involves torment. But he who fears has not been made perfect in love. – (1 John 4:18)

Spiritual warfare is very real. Look around you -the social unrest, the violence in our schools and in our streets, the persecution of Christians around the world (including here in the US), and the demoralizing of our society screams spiritual attacks from the devil and his minions. The devil is on the move and making great strides because he knows his time is short - *And war broke out in heaven: Michael and his angels fought with the dragon; and the dragon and his angels fought, but they did not prevail, nor was a place found for them in heaven any longer. So the great dragon was cast out, that serpent of old, called the Devil and Satan, who deceives the whole world; he was cast to the earth, and his angels were cast out with him.*

Then I heard a loud voice saying in heaven, "Now salvation, and strength, and the kingdom of our God, and the power of His Christ have come, for the accuser of our brethren, who accused them before our God day and night, has been cast down. And they overcame him by the blood of the Lamb and by the word of their testimony, and they did not love their lives to the death. Therefore rejoice, O heavens, and you who dwell in them! Woe to the inhabitants of the earth and the sea! For the devil has come down to you, having great wrath, because he knows that he has a short time." - (Rev. 12:7-12)

But know this: God has already won, He is Victorious. He has already Won the War and those who are in Christ have the Victory – IF They Claim It and Walk in It

Let these verses equip you for the battles to come:

For we wrestle not against flesh and blood, but against principalities, against powers, against the rulers of the darkness of this world, against spiritual wickedness in high places. ~Ephesians 6:12

Above all, taking the shield of faith, wherewith ye shall be able to quench all the fiery darts of the wicked. ~Ephesians 6:16

Be sober, be vigilant; because your adversary the devil, as a roaring lion, walketh about, seeking whom he may devour ~1st Peter 5:8

Submit yourselves therefore to God. Resist the devil, and he will flee from you. ~James 4:7

For whatsoever is born of God overcometh the world: and this is the victory that overcometh the world, even our faith. Who is he that overcometh the world, but he that believeth that Jesus is the Son of God? ~1st John 5:4-5

No weapon that is formed against thee shall prosper; and every tongue that shall rise against thee in judgment thou shalt condemn. This is the heritage of the servants of the Lord, and their righteousness is of me, saith the Lord. ~Isaiah 54:17

The Scriptures above are clear and to the point – we have the authority, we have the victory, we have everything we need to defeat the devil and everything he throws at us if we have the courage and the faith to believe God's Word enough to take action in our daily lives. Will you boldly walk out your faith today?

Praying for your enemies

Let's briefly discuss praying for your enemies especially since some reading this book may believe that President Trump is their enemy. There are several reasons that if you're a follower of Jesus Christ should pray for your enemies. First and foremost we have to guard against hatred and resentment building up within our spirit. Hatred and resentment is like a spiritual cancer that infects our spirit separating us from completing God's perfect will for our life. There is a fundamental Christian principle that Christ taught us and that is to be forgiven we have to forgive others – it's just that simple.

A lot of times when we do not forgive someone, in all reality it's only affecting us - the other person probably has no clue of the entirety of your feelings.

Let's once again look to the Scripture for clarification:

Matt. 5:43-47

"You have heard that it was said, 'You shall love your neighbor and hate your enemy.' But I say to you, love your enemies, bless those who curse you, do good to those who hate you, and pray for those who spitefully use you and persecute you, that you may be sons of your Father in heaven; for He makes His sun rise on the evil and on the good, and sends rain on the just and on the unjust. For if you love those who love you, what reward have you? Do not even the tax collectors do the same? And if you greet your brethren only, what do you do more than others? Do not even the tax collectors do so? Therefore you shall be perfect, just as your Father in heaven is perfect.

Rom. 12:9-21

Let love be without hypocrisy. Abhor what is evil. Cling to what is good. Be kindly affectionate to one another with brotherly love, in honor giving preference to one another; not lagging in diligence, fervent in spirit, serving the Lord; rejoicing in hope, patient in tribulation, continuing steadfastly in prayer; distributing to the needs of the saints, given to hospitality. Bless those who persecute you; bless and do not curse. Rejoice with those who rejoice, and weep with those who weep. Be of the same mind toward one another. Do not set your mind on high things, but associate with the humble. Do not be wise in your own opinion. Repay no one evil for evil. Have regard for good things in the sight of all men. If it is possible, as much as depends on you, live peaceably with all men. Beloved, do not avenge yourselves, but rather give place to wrath; for it is written, "Vengeance is Mine, I will repay," says the Lord.

Therefore "If your enemy is hungry, feed him; If he is thirsty, give him a drink; For in so doing you will heap coals of fire on his head." Do not be overcome by evil, but overcome evil with good.

Releasing this type of hatred, resentment, and unforgiveness cleanses your spirit as you repent of these things and enables you to draw closer to God. Additionally it eliminates the very feelings that those that practice the dark arts try to instill within those that follow God. Now this is not to say that there isn't a time and a place for righteous anger or even war. The Bible declares that you can be angry and not sin but you have to be led by the Word of God and His Holy Spirit.

Chapter 12:
Communicating to the President that we are Praying for Him

One of the number one threats to our freedom is what is known as the mainstream media. I would dare say that it is the number one threat to our way of life. President Trump has pointed out several times the bias of the mainstream media. In fact President Trump has even been so bold to proclaim some media outlets as fake news and very fake news respectively.

Sway the hearts and minds of the people and you will win the battle without firing a shot – this is the strategy of those that control the mainstream media outlets. It is very important to understand that the majority of the media outlets are controlled by just a handful of people.

In fact most of the mainstream media is owned by people that are not United States citizens. Personally I feel that it should be against the law to have foreigners own and control mainstream media outlets of any kind – this is a direct threat to our Republic. Additionally it should be noted here that the CIA and other intelligence agencies have worked with, infiltrated, and controlled specific news organizations in the past. This practice continues to this very day – and unfortunately it seems that the CIA and other Deep State agencies has gone rogue – So who are they really working for Now?

The First Amendment guaranteeing the freedom of the Press should not include foreign own media outlets in my humble opinion and the practice of attempting to control media outlets by the CIA and others should come to an immediate halt.

And if this isn't bad enough recently we find that White House Chief of Staff General Kelly stopped President Trump from getting information from Infowars.com and other alternative media sites. This ban also is in effect in the US Military as well.

More and more they are isolating President Trump from his core base – from you and me. Thankfully he still has his twitter account but they continue to attempt to isolate him from the truth. Why do you think that is? Is it a psychological operation to gain further control over President Trump?

We may not have all the answers to why it appears that they are isolating President Trump from his core base and from alternative media sources but one thing is for certain, a close society doesn't have a free press.

If the powers that be wish to pull off something big they need to have as much control as possible over news and media outlets – especially over those that they do not control such as alternative news sources like infowars.com.

Therefore it is critical for us to reach out to President Trump any way that we can weather it be social media platforms, physically writing letters, or going on YouTube and creating videos - he has to know that you and I are praying for him. He has to understand and know that he is not alone in his quest to "Make America Great Again"

Chapter 13: Conclusion

Thank you for reading our book, it is my hope and my prayer that you will take decisive action and put your faith into prayer for President Trump. Whether you're for him and his policies or against them, all of us here in the United States will benefit from praying for our President. If you are a "Never Trumper" I would still encourage you to lift up President Donald Trump in prayer, and if you consider him your enemy, all the more reason to pray for him.

The true intent of this book is to get you off the sidelines and into the game. We The People – do you remember these words? It's up to each one of us to stand in the gap in prayer daily if we really want to Make America Great Again

Special Gift

God has a Gift for You!   The Plan of
Salvation:

There is no formal prayer of salvation as
many churches would have you believe,
God's Word is very clear - there is only one
way to get to the Father in heaven and that
is through Jesus Christ (John 14:6). Jesus
says that you must be born again to enter
into heaven (John 3:3-5).

Salvation is simply the first step in building
an open and honest relationship with God.
We all have sinned and fallen short, but
there is Hope in Jesus Christ - Just cry out to
God in sincerity and honesty asking for
forgiveness and for Him to Save you,
Sanctify you, and fill you with His Holy Spirit
- Ask for His will to be done in your life on
earth as it is in Heaven and That's it, now
just keep it real with God.

A Warning:

The Christian walk is not an easy life on the surface. The Word of God says that we will be hated in all the world for Christ namesake (Matt. 24:9). The Bible says that in the last days are enemy prevail against us physically until Christ returns to save us (Dan 7:21, 22). Furthermore, we must endure hardship as a good soldier of Jesus Christ (2 Tim 2:3) and yet we are never alone in this, God promises us that He will never leave us nor forsake us if we believe in him (Matt.28:20).

In everything we go through we have the peace and joy of God which surpasses all understanding (Philp. 4:6-8) The Bible declares, "For I consider the sufferings of this present time are not worthy to be compared with the glory which shall be revealed in us". (Rom 8:18). However, in all these things we are more than conquerors through Jesus Christ (Rom. 8:37)

Stay In Contact

Our Contact Information

Stay in Contact with the American Christian Defense Alliance, Inc. through Our Website At: http://www.ACDAInc.Org

Join Our Mailing List

We also Greatly Appreciate You Signing Up For Our Mailing List and Providing a Good Rating and review for this Book. Your reviews help other people like yourself find this book on Amazon and benefit from its contents.

If You or Your Family have been Blessed by this book please let us know by dropping us a line through our website at http://acdainc.org

Find All Our Books

<u>Some of Our Books:</u>

Parenting: How To Be A Great Parent And
Raise Awesome Kids

Real Men Don't Make Promises:
Understanding Oaths, Pacts, Covenants &
Promises From A Biblical Perspective

Salvation for Your Unsaved Mom: 10 Things
to Tell Your Mom Before She Dies

The Perfection of Purity: A Message To My
Daughter

A Vague Notion: How To Overcome Limiting Beliefs of Fear and Anxiety Through the Word of God

Biblical Bug Out: Don't Bug In - Follow The Calling

Christian Prepping 101: How To Start Prepping

Martial Arts Ministry: How To Start A Martial Arts Ministry

Prepping: Survival Basics

How to Finance Your Full-Time RV Dream